Hitchhiking Beatitudes

Michael McInnis

Nixes Mate Books
Allston, Massachusetts

Copyright © 2017 Michael McInnis

Book design by d'Entremont
Cover photo from the collection of Lauren Leja

All rights reserved. This book or any portion thereof may not be reproduced or used in any manner whatsoever without the express written permission of the publisher except for the use of brief quotations in a book review or scholarly journal.

Special thanks to: Rusty Barnes, Philip Borenstein, Matt Borczon, Lauren Leja, Gloria Mindock, Annie Pluto and Jeff Weddle

ISBN 978-0-692-86923-9

Nixes Mate Books
POBox 1179
Allston, MA 02134
nixesmate.pub/books

The 'dictators' of the animal kingdom are those who live in an ambience of plenty. The anarchists, as always, are the 'gentlemen of the road'.
— Bruce Chatwin, *The Songlines*

Hitchhiking Beatitudes

We did a last line of crystal meth before my friend dropped me off outside of Escondido. No one will pick you up if they don't know where you're going, he said.

The Ayatollah, he said, we should bomb that country to shit. I envy you. Young and ready to go to war. But I only wanted to get to Imperial Beach to buy crystal meth.

I was 18, but looked 15: an old queer's lottery win.

I ate granola and apples and slept in wooded interchanges, menaced by mosquitoes, aware of the sky.

Smoking opium with the Australian surfers piloting a VW bus. UFOs flew over the salt pan, dislodged from hangars at Edwards Air Force base.

The desert sky reminded me of being at sea, a blanket of light, each star a tiny rock to be cut up, crushed and snorted.

The sun already hot. Another line of crystal and I could walk for miles. It felt like a thousand ants crawling across the swamp of my back, from shoulder blade to shoulder blade, always in a place where I could not scratch.

Beyond the globe of the van's headlights: Death Valley and the hot Mojave, last chance casinos and broken down relics, living ghost towns and the lights of the Strip, like a distant galaxy. Eighteen-inch trout. Best thing I ever ate, he said.

On the mountain meadow, I watched my parents murdered. All turned to white, scorching, luminous and dense like fog grappling with Point Loma.

I am a hoodoo, a red-painted soldier in the plateau's army where Ebenezer Bryce mustered us into a latter-day brigade. The Russian woman in gold slippers waited for nightfall, for the Red Army and 7,500 stars to scour the earth clean.

From the back of a pick up truck driven by an old Mormon and his wife, I smelled the great ocean recede. Their grandson stared at me, Moroni returned to America.

Utah was like driving on the moon, she said. New Zealand, where she was from, was like driving on another planet. She had traveled much further than me. I had yet to leave the stratosphere.

It all came back to Shiloh for John Wesley Powell. He buried his right arm at Shiloh and buried his nightmares on the Green River where dinosaurs still roam.

There was deep snow on the path leading up to the Medicine Wheel. An Indian walked counterclockwise, while bluebirds chanted. The summer sun so bright, I felt the mountain tremble as if I was back at sea.

The naked hippie walking down the road at Mesa Verde pointed to deer grazing next to my tent.

Llamas and buffalo loitered from Pine Ridge to Carhenge. A boy ran with a dog and threw a stick deep into the winter wheat.

Do not climb Devils Tower. Do not contact the aliens anchored above Devils Tower. Do not pet the prairie dogs, they are infested with bubonic plague. I touched the phonolite porphyry scree at the bottom of the tower. My right hand emits a hum.

Dull Knife and Little Wolf sold pottery at the Four Corners and collected tokens at Roadside America, Santa's Village and Wall Drug. We're all tourists in Indian Country now.

It only looks like I'm taking my pants off, he said. 3 million years ago, I sliced the Royal Gorge open with the edge of my hand.

Emmett Dalton and his brothers escaped down the tunnel beneath their sister's house in Meade. Dodge City looked like a ghost town. A silo emptied of grain quivered in the wind.

After the fire and death of Mamah at Taliesin, the shadow of Frank Lloyd Wright sat in a dark corner of his studio, cold and shuddering, erasing.

Graceland and Rowan Oak. I ate strawberries and heard the cries of the Tupelo dead.

The arch lit up as if a distant galaxy on the banks of the big muddy had imploded. Crossed the river in a wagon train. The Illiniwek in pursuit.

There were holes in the sky over Groom Lake, Trinity and inside the hangars of Wright-Patterson. Glass in the sand cut my feet.

He had driven a van full of live chickens all night and asked if I could drive a three on the tree. Every time I popped the clutch, it felt like a flightless bird had lurched into oblivion.

First the Anasazi clawed the earth, then the Alligewi.
It's illegal to take hallucinogens at the Serpent Mound.

In Mound City I spoke in tongues of fire: Chillicothe,
Tuscarora, Mahantango, Nescopeque, Poconos,
Susquehanna, Towanda, Mehoopany, Meshoppen,
Tunkhannock, Lackawanna, Equinumnk,
Wallenpaupack.

The state trooper said what are you doing on my fucking interstate. Thundering trucks, lit like alien Christmas trees, barreled out of the darkness.

On the road to Falling Water, the woman with spider eyes and a dozen silver balloons mustered in the backseat said, never buy chicken from a gas station and there is no mention in the Bible of radon – or, roosters on trampolines.

From the crest of Little Round Top I heard yellow jackets and minié balls crashing into trees, men mustered in lines, the crush of horses and smelled the earth open up, aflame, fragile, gasping. I witnessed the deconstruction of history.

I asked two women, sunbathing topless by a reservoir in Connecticut, if they had any reefer. We got high and I looked at their eyes.

Overhead, jetliners cry across an acrid blue sky. The sand is varnished with a slimy brown moss, broken bottles, tampons and plastic forks. At dawn the clamdiggers arrive, clutching coffees and pails, hacks and hoes.

If Plimoth Plantation were historically accurate, they would kill the leader of the local Indians and stick his head on a pole by the gate.

Thin yellow river ice of the Penobscot, menaced by the sun, drifted to the edge of the sea. On the banks of the river bent birch trees prayed to Mecca. I wished I was still on the Natchez Trace with Meriweather Lewis, both of us losing our minds.

In Rangley, Wilhelm Reich monitored the weather, cloud formations, temperature, humidity, deadly orgone radation and UFOs with cloudbusters.

The English burned Norridgewock, pissing on the ashes of the church that Peré Sebastion Rasles had built. When the Jesuit erected a new cross amidst the ruins, the English cut off his head and stuck it on his cross as a warning to Indians and Papists. The Indians now say they should have driven the English back into the sea.

Malsumi was Glooscap's evil twin, screaming in the wild. When I was tweaking, I heard his screaming through broken teeth, from inside stolen tanks, webbed within the toxic clouds of a meth lab explosion.

I waited for the trickster's return, for daylight to broadcast the screaming and howling in the distance. Black flies chewed necklaces across my collarbone.

Amphetamine-fueled drivers of logging trucks climbing the Whalesback on Route 9, never stopped at the lookout to see the glacial till, the drumlins, the eskers carving the surrounding bog. I scooped handfuls of wild blueberries.

Vagrancy in California. Vagrancy in Utah. Vagrancy in Newfoundland. Vagrancy in Sedalia, Missouri. Vagrancy in Shiloh and Antietam. All that bloodshed set the continent on fire. On the Plains of Abraham I lost my history.

My grandparents spoke a secret American language.
Je ne parle pas Française Acadien.

The men of Quebec had wandering hands and after they asked where I was headed, asked if I liked boys or girls.

Outside Pointe-au-Pére, touching my face and hair was the only language I shared with four high-school girls. I wanted to spend my life with them and reclaim my heritage.

The Gaspé Peninsula is the tailbone of the Appalachian Mountains. The Mi'kmaq called it *gespe'g*, the end, the edge of the world, where Glooscap, the trickster creator kept a hunting lodge.

After the woman who had lived with the Cree invited me into her house for a *drink of water*, I headed south past Percé Rock where the traveling salesman picked me up.

The traveling salesman asked me why I carried a knife. At a restaurant everyone stared at us because I looked like Anglophile rough trade and he looked like respectable Quebecois.

You were so hard and beautiful while you slept, he said,
I came three times.

In Cape Breton, Alexander Graham Bell found
Scotland all over again in the hills and fingers of Bras
d'Or. The Indians cluttered the road, drunk and riled up
because an English had run over a young Mi'kmaq boy.

On the ferry from Nova Scotia to Newfoundland, I was the only one in line for food. Even the cooks were seasick.

In Newfoundland, to appease the rocks and rivers, to placate the trees and lichen, to honor the stars screaming across the sky, I stripped and came on the stomach of the earth.

At l'Anse aux Meadows, the icebergs waited ten thousand years for a longship, the wind divorced from the sky.

The last full-blooded Beothuk, the original "red Indians", died in 1829. The Latecomers continue to leave the island to ghosts and priests holding empty plates.

Michael McInnis lives in Boston and served six years in the Navy chasing white whales and Soviet submarines. He was the founder of the Primal Plunge, Boston's first and only bookstore dedicated to zine and underground culture and small press literature. When he is not writing, Michael spends his time making furniture and composing ambient soundtrack music. His poetry and short fiction has appeared or is forthcoming in *Chiron Review, The Commonline Journal, Cream City Review, Naugatuck Review, One-Sentence Poems, Oxford Magazine, White Knuckle Press* and *Yellow Chair Review* to name a few.

Nixes Mate is a navigational hazard in Boston Harbor first used by colonists to graze their sheep. The island became infamous after the bodies of convicted pirates were gibbetted there to serve as warnings to mutinous sailors.

Nixes Mate Books features small-batch artisanal literature, created by writers that use all 26 letters of the alphabet and then some, honing their craft the time-honored way: one line at a time.

More Nixes Mate titles:
ON BROAD SOUND | Rusty Barnes
KINKY KEEPS THE HOUSE CLEAN | Mari Deweese
SQUALL LINE ON THE HORIZON | Pris Campbell
COMES TO THIS | Jeff Weddle

Forthcoming titles from Nixes Mate:
LUBBOCK ELECTRIC | Anne Elezabeth Pluto
NIXES MATE REVIEW ANTHOLOGY 2016/17
STORIES | Lauren Leja

nixesmate.pub/books

www.ingramcontent.com/pod-product-compliance
Lightning Source LLC
Chambersburg PA
CBHW051958290426
44110CB00015B/2292